A PLACE THEY CALLED
AMERICA

A PLACE THEY CALLED
AMERICA

WILLIAM PANZARELLA

Book design by Maureen Cutajar
www.gopublished.com

ISBN: 978-1-329-40507-3

Contents

"Freedom is never more than one generation away from extinction. We didn't pass it to our children in the bloodstream. It must be fought for, protected, and handed on for them to do the same."

—Ronald Reagan

The Oligarchy

I was originally going to write a novel about America in the "not so distant future", where the Constitution has been torn apart, where the government spies on our every move, where citizens live in fear of saying or writing certain things, where the younger generation has been brainwashed, where citizens are mere slaves to those in control. But then I realized that future is now. Plans set in motion some time ago, to destroy democracy and control the population, have come to fruition. No, this is not yet the end result. The plan is still unfolding. But we are in the final stages of the eradication of the American Dream and the Constitution as we know it. If an American had been in a coma for the past twenty-five years and woke up today, they would find the United States, its principles, values, and vision unrecognizable. They would find it little different than some of the tyrannies they had fought to end.

So if these elaborate and diabolical plans have been envisioned and put into place than who are the architects and what is their end game? For as long as their have been governments their have been those in power, or who have coveted power, who see themselves as demigods and whish to not only control their peoples, but to have their peoples serve their every needs. It was true with the Pharos, it was true with the Roman

1

Emperors, it was true with Monarchs, it was true with Stalin, Mao, and Hitler and it is true today. But what makes these modern-day rulers dangerous is not that they share the brutality of their predecessors, but rather that they have learned from their mistakes.

The term oligarchy is usually used in reference to Russia. But there are those that wish to turn—and have already turned into a certain extent—America, and the entire world, into an oligarchy. These people, these self-proclaimed demigods, consist of those in the highest stratosphere of power and influence. By no means do I believe that every politician fits into this category. Some that serve in Congress, and at more local levels, actually do have the best interest of the country in their hearts (or at least they did when they started). Even those politicians that fall in line and help implement this master plan many are mere pawns. Many of those who are at the top of the pyramid are officially not in government—though they use the government as their sword—but are part of the elite, the most wealthy and influential, those who yield absolute power. They consist of the puppet masters who control the puppets, who in turn control the rest of us. Again, I want to make myself clear. In no way am I saying that everyone who is a billionaire or in a capacity of power has nefarious intentions or is part of some conspiracy. Not only do I believe in capitalism and being able to make as much money as you can, but there are many extremely wealthy people who not only respect the principles of our country, but have done great deeds for its people. There are those running successful and affluent companies that, although have probably had to make some very difficult decisions, want democracy and the American dream to prosper. There are also powerful companies that produce vital goods and services, including the securing of our homeland.

But the Oligarchy is real and is gaining power day by day, and has set their sights on nothing short of world domination. They are not just about the uber-elite making more money. They already have more money than they can ever spend. It is about power. But as they gain power, the People lose their power, their liberties, and their Constitutional rights. They are a tyranny and we are here merely to serve them.

It is not only America that they want to control and it is not only Americans who consist of this exclusive and arcane consortium. Perhaps the greatest device to their plan has been globalization. There is absolutely no argument that with implementation of global conglomerates and the omnipresence of the Internet the world, despite its rapidly growing population, is more connected and smaller than it has ever been. Unfortunately, as the world consolidates, so does the Oligarchy's power.

But though this ultimately is a plan of global dominance, it starts with, and cannot succeed without, the destruction of the pumping heart of freedom—America. Here in America the Oligarchy is alive and well, conniving and executing its elaborate plans. Behind closed doors they decide what is to become of all our lives. We may vote on our leaders, often the lesser of two evils, but with rare exceptions do we vote on the laws that govern every aspect of our lives. The Oligarchy and their henchmen operate with complete impunity. Even if they are caught doing something untoward they spin the truth, create diversions and misinformation, and buy their way out of trouble. Even in the rare instances where someone must be held accountable they throw to the wolves a sacrificial lamb, a scapegoat.

Many politicians are mere Manchurian candidates. They are beholden to those that put them in power and both sides of the isle are guilty of this. The highest echelon of powerbrokers contributes to the campaigns of politicians, from the state level up to the Presidency. Many are at the upper crust of Wall Street and despite the great lie that it is only the Republican Party that is intertwined with these elitists, many of the top Wall Street names, such as George Soros and Warren Buffett, give money to and support candidates of the Democratic Party. But it is certainly far from Wall Street fat cats that contribute to the campaigns and careers of American politicians. Foreign persons, entities, and even countries help candidates win elections. There are laws and regulations regarding who can contribute to a campaign. But with every rule there are ways around it. Many times, instead of giving money directly to the campaign, these persons and entities give money to foundations that are controlled by the candidates. But even if they give directly to campaigns, only the most naive person would believe the amount of money that is publically reported.

There are numerous foreign entities and peoples to which our highest government officials are beholden and most remain, or at least try to remain, secret. However, there can be no denying that the Saudi Royal Family has great power and influence over the tip of our government's spear—the President and the White House. They have for some time and although much of the Oligarchy works in the shadows, perhaps no entity overtly represents it than the Saudi Family. America has bent over backwards for them, fought wars for them, turned a blind eye to their deeds and tyrannical oppression, and aided them at times even at the cost to American citizens. To be clear, this tie has spanned presidencies of both parties.

Just as destructive to America's interest is those members of the Oligarchy that are from, or have great investments in, China. Just as beholden the United States is to the Saudis, we are beholden to China. With each passing year more of America is being parceled out to the Chinese. Moguls of Chinese industry continue to purchase, at an alarming rate, commercial and private real estate, as well as businesses throughout the United States. Also, American-based companies are virtually prostituting themselves to the Chinese government in order to get their foot in the door of the expanding Chinese economy. China has also become the United State's bank, holding more U.S. debt than any other country. This would be a dangerous proposition even for an ally. But despite our business and financial relationship, China is no ally of America. Unlike Saudi Arabia, they possess a true military threat to the United States and that threat is only growing rapidly as they expand all facets of their military. Furthermore, China is the greatest cyber threat to America, actively committing cyber warfare on our country everyday. In June of 2015 U.S. officials blamed China for hacking into some of the most sensitive government systems and stealing personal, including classified, information of four million federal employees in what experts say is to create a massive database for the purpose of blackmail and espionage. Our government calls them out and rattles its saber, but can do little else because of China's involvement in the Oligarchy and their ties to those in the U.S. government and industry.

With that said, there is no more powerful master to American politicians, and no greater mechanism for the Oligarchy and their plans, than the lobbyist. Lobbying firms are clandestine and work on anonymity and secrecy. The vast majority of citizens cannot name a single lobbyist or even a lobbying firm. Yet they are the backbone, not only to putting a candidate office, but keeping him or her there. However, this is less about giving actual money, though it is ludicrous to think that cash and assets do not change hands in under-the-table deals. Lobbyists work more on a quid pro quo basis. It is said that in organized crime never ask someone for a favor because you will owe that favor back tenfold. Well, many of the men and women who run our government make the most notorious organized crime members envious.

Though the Oligarchy, either through its members or marionettes, spread their propaganda through all aspects of media, their truest intentions are devised in secrecy. Sometimes it is through small face-to-face meetings and conversations. Other times it is through larger, more elaborate gatherings. They always try to either keep these conferences completely covert or label them something benign, in case the public gets wind from truth-seekers, whose voices are constantly trying to be silenced and/or discredited.

One of the most infamous, though still obscure, of these meetings is the annual Bilderberg Group conference. Each year, since 1954, some of the most powerful figures in the world meet in the Netherlands. Over time the meetings have become public knowledge. The Bilderberg Group now even has its own official website, which states that the annual conferences are designed to "foster dialogue between Europe and North America". Some of the 2014 attendees included: Keith B. Alexander, former Commander of U.S. Cyber Command and Director of the NSA; Robert E. Rubin, former Secretary of the U.S. Treasury; Eric E. Schmidt, Executive Chairman of Google; Stephen S. Poloz, Governor of the Bank of Canada; Fleur Pellerin, France's State Secretary of Foreign Trade; Paul M. Achleitner, Chairman of the Supervisory Board of Deutsche Bank AG; and Anders Fogh Rasmussen, Secretary General of NATO; among many other powerbrokers from countries all over the world. Among the topics discussed at the 2014 meeting, according to the group's website: Does privacy exist; The new architecture of the Middle East; and the Future of democracy. Again, that is according to their own website. However, no media of any kind is allowed into the meeting and no transcripts are disseminated. Exactly what was discussed is a closely guarded secret.

Of course, there are also other infamous secret societies, such as the Free Masons and Knights Templars, which have been around for hundreds of years and have been the topic of countless books, movies, and documentaries.

But there are other, even more clandestine societies, which operate in the complete shadows. There are meetings and conferences that go on all the time around the world of which the public has little or no knowledge.

Though the Oligarchy's tentacles spread around the globe and they wish to control all countries, under the guise of a New World Order, in order to control the world, you must control the United States.

The great General and then President Dwight D. Eisenhower was quoted as saying: "Here in America we are descended in blood and spirit from revolutionists and rebels—men and women who dare to dissent from accepted doctrine". He was right. Though history confirms that America has had its times of wrong and regret, in its spirit, in its founding principle and Constitution, is the belief and realization of freedom. If anything may compromise that freedom, may We The People stand up and fight until the bitter end. Democracy is not just governance, but the idea, the mantra, that it is better to die fighting than to succumb and give up those freedoms. As Patrick Henry famously coined: "Give me liberty or give me death."

So than how is any oligarchy, any tyranny, able to achieve its ultimate goal of controlling a free and rebellious society such as the United States? In order for any tyranny to be implemented and have long-term success it must do four things: 1) Indoctrinate the youth; 2) Divide and conquer; 3) Control the supply of goods and services; 4) Disarm the populace; and 5) Spy on and monitor the citizens. But this especially implies to a nation of mass territory and a massive population and it is the only way that it can ever happen in America.

It is a process. The Oligarchy cannot come in and take all of your rights and freedoms at once. If it did it would have to be done by overwhelming force and would surely be met with a massive resistance.

Their plan is to take our rights little-by-little, tear the Constitution bit-by-bit. If you have a large jar of coins and one night someone took half the jar you would notice right away. But if someone steals a handful of coins at a time, over an extended period, you may not realize until it is too late. Make no mistake the jar is now more than half empty. As I stated previously, the Oligarchy's plan is already in its final stages.

Indoctrination

The first and most important step to the success of any tyranny is the indoctrination of the youth. The youth are the future and in order to control the future, you must control the youth. But you cannot simply do it by force. If you control someone by force they can always form a resistance and eventually fight back. But if you brainwash them, they will not even realize that they are being controlled.

The first step to indoctrination starts with the brainwashing of students in school, as early as Kindergarten, though it earnestly begins in elementary school. In order to indoctrinate you must destroy the individual. With individualism comes questions, opinions, and even rebellion—all enemies of indoctrination and control. The goal is to have everyone conform into a collective way of thinking. To do this you must start the process even before boys and girls begin to come into their own way of thinking and expressing themselves.

In Nebraska, Lincoln Public schools are pushing to ban teachers from saying "boys" and "girls" in an effort to eliminate even the individualism of genders. But that is just a microcosm of what is rapidly spreading in school districts across our nation.

Of course, the pillar of individualism, as well as our Constitution's

First Amendment, is the right to free speech. It is the inalienable right to voice one's own opinions without being punished or silenced. However, dissenting opinions are not tolerated in many of our schools today. I'm not talking about a student questioning a math equation or even scientific method. Teachers and professors have specific political views and they often penalize and even ridicule students that turn in papers or give speeches that oppose those views in any way, no matter how well researched and articulate the student presents those views.

Then, of course, there is the war on Christianity, but specifically Christmas. Christmas is still a national holiday. Yet in many grade schools and high schools Christmas parties and events are no longer allowed, instead replaced by generic holiday parties. Though it goes well beyond parties and events. In many schools Christmas trees are not allowed. There have been countless stories of children having to take cookies and cupcakes they brought to school home because they have a cross or Christmas tree on them. Not only in schools, but in society at large, we are being told that the mere greeting Merry Christmas is not "politically correct" and we should instead just say Happy Holidays. But how does this equate to indoctrination? Because when you want people to be brainwashed and only regurgitate what they are taught than you have to remove faith and the belief that there is a higher power. Naturally though, this cannot be the reason given for the erosion of Christmas. Instead, it is blamed on a mere handful of lawsuits from atheists.

Eradicating faith is just one facet of indoctrination. In controlling a nation, especially the United States, indoctrination does not only mean to conform to a new way of thinking, but in order to shape the mind, it means to rewrite history. This is done by cementing the idea that America has been evil and has always been on the wrong side of history. If America has been a beckoning sign of hope than no one, not even a young mind, would want to change her. So America must be turned into the great villain.

Certainly, America has had its black marks—the way Native Americans were treated, slavery, Jim Crow—and these things should be taught in school. In telling history you must tell the truth, the good, the bad, and the ugly. You cannot run from it or pretend it never happened. It must be taught as a lesson so that we may learn from it. But despite its shameful dark moments, America has not only more often than not been on the right side of history, but she has more than once saved the world from oppression. Since World War I, time and time again it has been the United States who has been called upon foremost to save countless other countries from conflict and natural disasters. However, the truth of America as a savior and land of hope is being erased from our schools.

If history is being re-written, and the idea that America is evil is being taught in elementary and high schools, than it is being taken to the next level in our colleges. If elementary and high schools are basic training than our universities have become Special Forces training for indoctrination.

More than ever, in order to get a good job in this country you need a college degree. In the past this was because if you had a college degree it meant that you obtained more pertinent knowledge, were more intelligent and in theory I agree with this. Higher education is something that should be sought. Not only as individuals, but as a nation, we need brighter minds, we need engineers and scientists, entrepreneurs and inventors. The problem is that today, the powers that be want a college degree to be required because it means, in many cases, that the indoctrination has been complete. All across the country college classrooms, lecture halls, and campuses are awash with the most anti-American and anti-democracy propaganda imaginable. In fact, that is the number one thing being taught in our universities.

Ward Churchill was a professor at the University of Colorado Boulder from 1990 to 2007 and has also given lectures at other colleges. In his books, speeches, and interviews Churchill professes and teaches his disdain for America. After the attacks of September 11, 2001 he wrote: "The men who flew the missions against the WTC and Pentagon were not cowards." He called the victims of 9/11 "Little Eichmanns", referring to Adolf Eichmann, one of Hitler's main coordinators of the Holocaust. However, he also decries America's role in WWII and routinely claims that the United States has committed numerous genocides.

Another proud anti-American that has influenced countless college students is Bill Ayers, co-founder of the Weather Underground, a domestic terrorist group that bombed the New York City Police headquarters, the Capitol, and the Pentagon in the early seventies. Even to this day Ayers proclaims his hatred towards America. Besides writing extremist books and having political influence, he was a professor at the University of Illinois from 1987-2010 and in 2008 Ayers was elected as Vice president for Curriculum Studies at the American Educational Research Association. He also routinely gives speeches at numerous universities.

College professors and lecturers are not only teaching students that America is evil, but the students are listening. In 2015, students at the University of California, Irvine voted to ban the American Flag on campus. At the Valdosta State University in Georgia, students and others protested America by walking on the American flag. Then, when Air Force veteran Michelle Manhart forcefully took the flag from them and refused to give it back, she was arrested by the university police.

In September 2014, as an experiment, reporter Dan Johnson videoed himself on the campus of George Mason University asking students to sign a petition supporting the terrorist army ISIS. In the first hour he was able to get over a dozen signatures. However, not all students that signed did so because they were anti-American; some did so blindly, not even realizing what they were signing. Some students had no idea what ISIS was. They say ignorance is bliss, but it is also extremely dangerous. It might be surprising to many that college students had no clue about ISIS seeing how the terrorist group was the main story of almost every media outlet at the time. But this ignorance is no accident. Part of the indoctrination taking place now is not merely programing the mind with certain information, but it is also about the eroding and blindness of certain knowledge. The more stupid people are, the less well informed they are, the easier it is to lead them like sheep to the slaughter.

In my previous book, More Common Sense, I have a chapter titled: The Dumbing Of America. The deliberate plan to make the nation's populace stupid has been in motion for a long time and gains speed with each passing year. Everyone is entitled to some mindless entertainment and there is nothing wrong with that. But it should be a small supplement of life, not the main source of thinking. There are countless young adults throughout America that can tell you which celebrities are dating who and name all of the Housewives of New Jersey, but cannot name the Secretary of State or even the Vice-President. There are countless people across the nation that can tell you detail-by-detail what is occurring on a particular reality show but cannot tell you what is going on in the Middle East or point to Saudi Arabia on a map. These are the people that are going to vote to elect our leaders. Many of these people will become teachers, agents of the government, and obtain other positions that influence our lives. Not only are the ignorant easier to lead and sculpt, but they are easier to become spreaders of propaganda.

So you can see, indoctrination is not just happening in our schools and although the youth of America is the primary target, naturally the powers that be want it to encompass as many people as possible. For both the youth and older populace the propaganda of Hollywood, as well as the mainstream media, is vital to the overall plan. Sometimes it is overt, other times it is quite subliminal.

But why would Hollywood and the mainstream media want to propagate and create a society that is anti-American? First and foremost, many actors, directors, and producers actually believe that America is villainous and is the cause of most of the world's troubles and suffering. They blind themselves to the fact that the United States gives more aid to impoverished nations than any other country, or that when calamities strike, like the earthquake in Haiti, the tsunami in Indonesia, or the tsunami and earthquake in Japan, it is the U.S. military that is often first on the scene to rescue victims, provide relief, and help in the recovery, or that during genocides like what happened in Serbia, it was America who came to the aid of Muslims and others. The majority of those in Hollywood never bring these facts up because it would make it much harder to help indoctrinate and implant the idea that America is *always* the villain.

So than the question becomes why are they so anti-American? Many of them, along with many in the media, were indoctrinated themselves, products of first and second-generation brainwashing born out of the sixties. Shining examples of how deceiving this indoctrination is, many of the hippies who preached free speech and anti-establishment became some of the most intolerant people imaginable, stifling any dissent and free speech if it goes against what they believe. As far as proudly being anti-establishment, they became the establishment. Many of them became Hollywood and media moguls and passed down their extreme, stringent beliefs to their children and no place is more of a family affair than Hollywood.

As for why the media would want to play a part, not only in indoctrination, but also causing discord, pitting Americans against each other, there are several reasons. First of all, conflict sells and news corporations are in the business of selling. There is nothing they hate more than peace and harmony. Secondly, like many of their Hollywood brethren, there are national pundits and reporters, some who have their own news shows, that truly disdain America and its founding principles, such as the Constitution.

There is also nepotism between those in the media and the government and other powers. Al Sharpton, who has his own news show on MSNBC, is an adviser to President Obama. Claire Shipman, who is a contributor for ABC News and before that covered the White House for CNN, is married to Jay Carney, President Obama's former White House Press Secretary. Some campaign and even cabinet members—of both parties—become members of the media after their political careers. But once they become reporters and anchors there is a perception that they will become unbiased and that their political affiliations have been severed. George Stephanopoulos served as President Bill Clinton's Senior Advisor for policy and strategy. Later, he became a news anchor for ABC and even the host of one of their flagship news programs, This Week, as well as co-hosting Good Morning America. Presenting himself as an objective journalist, it was uncovered in 2015 that he had given $75,000 to the Clinton Foundation, a fact that he failed to disclose. He also did not disclose that he had been a moderator at several Clinton Global Initiative meetings while he was working for ABC. But surely these examples are the tip of the iceberg. Most of the ties between reporters and politicians, administrations, and major companies we may never know.

Prominent members in the media are beholden to politicians and power-players, thus making unbiased reporting impossible. I am not referring to shows on news outlets that clearly represent themselves as being editorial and opinion-driven; I am referring to those that represent themselves as bipartisan and strictly reporting the news.

Indoctrination is not only to brainwash citizens. Those being indoctrinated today, in grade schools, high schools, and colleges, will be tomorrow's police officers, service members, and federal agents. And they will be more apt to turn their guns on their own citizens if and when the order comes down. The bedrock that the Nation belongs to the People is being erased in schools and much of pop culture and thus their allegiance will strictly be to the government no matter what the government orders them to do.

Divide and Conquer

The media, Hollywood, and government also all come together to help implement the second part of the Oligarchy's plan: To divide and conquer.

Just because you are for one thing does not always mean that you are diametrically opposed to the other. I believe everything must be put on a scale and sometimes the pros only slightly outweigh the cons. You can understand someone's point of view but still disagree with it. However, this way of thinking is being eradicated and replaced with the notion that if you agree with X, than you must hate Y. There is no scale. There is no middle ground. Everything is black and white, figuratively, and quite often, literally. If you turn on the news, or listen to a politician, so much of today's discord and problems have to do with race.

I am not naïve enough to think that racism no longer exists at all in America, or any society. Racism and prejudice are born out of ignorance and hate and as long as there is an ounce or ignorance and hate left in society there will be racism and prejudice. But thankfully America has come a long, long way since the days of Jim Crow. Charles Manson's dream of creating a great, national race war had become the sick bygone fantasy of an evil, demented mind. However, there are prominent politicians and media members that seem to be bringing back Manson's deranged vision into a possibility.

The plan to divide America, especially along racial lines, reached a new height when Barack Obama first ran for President. Not because he was African-American, but because anyone that criticized him in any way was labeled a racist by his minions. It was a deliberate strategy. In affect, the tens of millions of people who did not vote for him were designated racists. It is difficult to get more divisive than that. Perhaps there was a very small segment of the population that did not vote for him because he was black. But to insinuate that every white person that disagrees with him is doing so because he is black is radical propaganda. Even if prominent black people disagree with Obama, such as ex-Congressman Allen West, radio host David Webb, or Supreme Court Justice Clarence Thomas, they are labeled Uncle Toms. Any Latino that disagrees with him is marginalized to the point that their voices are silenced.

Though Obama may have been a focal point, the racial division in this country now runs much deeper. It seems as if any time there is a crime committed by a white person against a black person, or a white person against a Latino, or even a Latino against a black person, as happened in the tragic Trayvon Martin case, the mainstream media and celebrity race-baiters make a nuclear mushroom cloud out of it. I want to be extremely clear—a single crime by anyone against someone else because of his or her ethnicity is abhorrent and should not be tolerated. I am also not saying that it should not be reported. However, there are horrific crimes committed by blacks against whites and Latinos against whites and blacks against Latinos and Latinos against Asians and so on nearly everyday. Surely not all of these are committed because of the victims' race, but some are.

Also, there is a tragic epidemic of black-on-black crimes in America, mostly due to gang violence, which today is a much larger and more dangerous problem than racism. But the mainstream media routinely whitewashes this because it does not fit the narrative.

Some people believe, and are trying to propagate, the idea that even if Caucasians are not racist today, they should pay for the crimes committed by their ancestors, such as slavery. Actor and comedian Chris

18

Rock said that all white people today should have to pay for slavery. First off, I believe that sons should never have to pay for the sins of their father. Let's also be clear, no one alive today has ever owned a slave. Furthermore, people like Chris Rock discard the fact that hundreds of thousands of young white men fought and died to abolish slavery.

Thankfully, despite what is being propagated by the mainstream media and others, we have come a long way in our race relations in America—as we should. It is despicable that there should be anywhere on the planet where people are treated differently because of the shade of their skin. Yet many people are trying to exploit the ugliness of racism to help to divide and conquer. People like the Reverend Al Sharpton and Jessie Jackson have made lifelong careers as race-baiters, causing hate and discord instead of trying to bring people together.

But people like Sharpton and Jackson would not have the influence that they do if the media did not give them the platform. The media is perhaps the greatest engine of division, acting like a hatchet upon society. Their main catalyst to divide and conquer is through the two-party system of government. Using "experts", politicians, and TV and radio hosts they have pitted Republicans against Democrats like never before—and it is not just about race. Enter "The War on Women". They are doing their part to cement the idea that all Republicans are not only racist, but also sexist. Of course, the truth is there have been Republican women in Congress, as well as African-Americans. There is even Mia Love from Utah, a black Congresswoman, who is Republican. However, the media purposely glosses over this fact because, again, it does not fit the narrative of divisiveness that they are trying to push. Today, more than any ideological or political differences, it is along perceived racial and gender lines that pit Democrats against Republicans, thus splitting the country apart.

The Oligarchy, through its influences and ties with the media and Hollywood, proliferate this strategy of divide and conquer by giving race-baiters platforms, spreading disinformation, and working the populace into a frenzy. Why? Because if the People are fighting each other than they have less time and energy to fight against the true enemy. Their attention is diverted away from the most dangerous and imminent threat to our nation, the taking away of our rights and the destruction of the Constitution. Abraham Lincoln had famously said: "A house divided against itself cannot stand". The Oligarchy is counting on this and is doing everything in its power to make sure it happens.

The Control of Goods
and Services

I want to be crystal clear, as I stated previously, I believe in capitalism. I believe in supply and demand. I believe in the free market system. However, anyone that has spent any time living on their own, paying bills, trying to get ahead, knows that the game is fixed.

The fact is that Wall Street is the greatest enemy to capitalism and free markets. There is not a single major financial firm that hasn't been caught—multiple times—fixing various rates and defrauding consumers. Insider trading, Ponzi schemes, phantom structured products, and fixing prices are all the complete opposite of what capitalism is supposed to be. Wall Street is the manipulation of free markets. Though in certain instances they can make a fortune and take advantage of downturns in the markets, for the most part, the Oligarchy does not want the markets to crash. They may always hedge their bets, partially protecting them against certain losses, but the vast majority of the time they profit when the world equities, fixed income, and commodities indexes go up. The problem is just because a sector goes up does not mean it is a good thing. Sure, it is good for the investors, but sometimes it is detrimental to the overall public.

The Oligarchy exerts its power over the populace by controlling specific, albeit vital, good and services. There is no more obvious good that represents this than oil. If the price of automobiles, computers, or televisions goes up it can be a great inconvenience, but people can get by. But oil is needed to run the world, especially an advanced civilization such as America. Not only does oil refine to gas, which powers all our cars to get us to and from work and everywhere else we need to go, but it powers all the trucks and diesel locomotives that transport every product that we use, including food. Without this transportation society as we know it would shut down. Petroleum is also used in the manufacture of countless products.

This is where the Saudi Royal Family comes into play. They do not want America to be energy efficient. They want America to depend on OPEC, because many members of the Oligarchy are either part of the leadership of OPEC or are in partnership with them. But there would be a great backfire if the Saudis and the rest of OPEC said they want America always to have to depend on their oil. So they no doubt covertly funnel massive money into U.S. environmental groups that help spread the notion that drilling for oil and natural gas inside of America and off her shores is not only dangerous, but almost evil.

Though America has enough oil it can drill to make us almost completely energy independent, lobbyists, governmental agencies, and media-fueled protest groups stop much of it from happening. Even financial experts on the news help try to convince the public that American oil independence is not exactly in our best interest by ludicrously claiming that low oil prices are actually a bad thing. To be sure, low oil prices are a negative for them and their wealthy friends on Wall Street that have stake in oil companies. Naturally low oil prices are also a negative for the oil companies and the people that work for them— not just the hierarchy, but also the hard working rank-and-file. However, whereas low oil prices may adversely affect 5% of the population, they greatly benefit the other 95%.

But even with constant and powerful opposition, companies do drill and refine oil in the United States. Even within the Oligarchy there is a constant power struggle and money grab. Yet in the end, though there may be skirmishes, they ultimately set their differences aside for the betterment of the whole, because just like the Mafia's Commission, they know they can make more money and have more power if they work together.

Oil, perhaps more than any other subject, also brings up the notion of American imperialism; that America wants to rule the world. People say the only reason we have fought in the Middle East is to control all the oil. This is a farce. If this was true, to the victor goes the spoils and after liberating Kuwait the U.S. government would have insisted on owning part of their oil fields, or we would own some of the oil fields in Iraq and elsewhere. Not to mention, we would drill enough oil in our homeland so that we would never have to be beholden to the Middle East. But it is not about American imperialism. It is not solely an American oligarchy; it is a global oligarchy. So we may fight over oil, but it is not so the United States can control it, but rather so the global oligarchy, in which there are Americans, can control it.

When it comes to goods and services, just as important as oil, is healthcare and prescription medication. But even more than oil, this is where the American people are victimized and are at the mercy of multi-billion dollar conglomerates. According to the World Health Organization, as of 2013, the United States lagged behind thirty-four other countries in life expectancy, despite spending the most per person on healthcare.

It is common knowledge that the main reason for America's poor healthcare (in relation to the money spent on it) is the fleecing of patients from insurance companies, hospitals, pharmaceutical companies, and government entities. Insurance companies, hospitals, and other medical facilities can, and do, charge whatever they want in the United States. Specific to prescription medication, pharmaceutical companies say the reason some medication is so astronomically expensive is because it costs so much to manufacture. However, that does not explain why they send those exact same medications to other countries and sell them for a fraction of the price. They force Americans to pay outrageous prices because they know they can get away with it.

Of course, lobbyists, once again, come into play. Despite every politician promising to fix healthcare in America, including President Obama and his Affordable Care Act, the average cost of healthcare, including medication, keeps skyrocketing at a rate many times above any inflation rate. That is because, like so many other things that affect our everyday lives, lobbyists and members of the Oligarchy trump everything else, including our health.

Though the control of healthcare services affects every American, usually the ones victimized the most are the sickest and elderly. A logical conclusion could be that is because they require the most care and thus produce the highest medical bills. That is unfortunately true. However, there are also other reasons. Specific to the elderly, they have paid into Medicare for most of their lives. That should mean now that they need those benefits it should be there for them. But Medicare is an enormous governmental expense. In fact, healthcare, of which Medicare is a major part, takes up approximately 25% of all federal spending. The government is happy when people are paying in, but turns around and laments when they have to pay it out. Many politicians want to do away with Medicare altogether. That is why some are content with the elderly, who have paid the most into it, dying off before they need to use what is rightfully theirs.

An even more insidious reason that the Oligarchy would not mind if not only the elderly, but even people who are fifty, sixty-years-old, die off is that these people are more apt to resist and try to stop the efforts to destroy the democracy. Most of these individuals are past the point of being able to be indoctrinated.

The Disarming of America

I f you want to control the populace than obviously you want to take away their ability to fight back, or at least minimize it as much as you possibly can. It is no secret that for some time there has been an all-out effort to eradicate the Constitution's Second Amendment. Just for the record, the Second Amendment states: "A well regulated militia, being necessary to the security of a free state, the right of the people to keep and bare arms, shall not be infringed." That's it. It is not some long, convoluted text up to interpretation. It does not say that the right of the People to bare arms shall not be abolished; it states that it "shall not be infringed" at all. Yet it has time and time again.

Of course, the government cannot just come out and say they want to take away every law-abiding citizens legally acquired firearms, or even the mere right, granted under the Second Amendment to acquire fire-arms, because they want the populace to be disarmed. So they do it under the guise that guns are evil, anyone that owns a gun is evil and morally corrupt, and if we don't take away all the guns we are heading towards killing fields on the streets of America where no man, woman, or child is safe. Those in the government that are pedaling this propa-ganda are doing so with the help of the mainstream media and

Hollywood. In listening to them you would think that guns are the only way people are killed. On September 11, 2001, terrorists killed 2,977 people in New York, Washington D.C., and Pennsylvania. Not a single one of the terrorists used a gun. Timothy McVeigh blew up an entire building and killed 168 people in Oklahoma without using a gun. But the fact remains that people are killed everyday in this country by guns. However, the vast majority of the time it has absolutely nothing to do with gun laws.

When politicians and so-called experts talk about "American gun laws" it is a misnomer. Yes, there are federal gun laws. But more often than not people are mostly affected by their State, or even city, gun laws. Some places in the United States have laws that are more different to each other than many countries. For instance, places like Chicago and New York City have tougher gun laws than many countries. Even the entire State of New York has completely stricter and different gun laws than Arizona or Nebraska. New York and other states have gun laws that are in fact, much stricter than the federal statutes.

Often, the places within the country with the toughest firearms laws are those that have the highest gun homicide rates. Perfect examples of this are Chicago and Camden, New Jersey. But even in places that have less strict gun laws, in the overwhelming majority of the cases, gun violence is committed by criminals who acquired guns illegally. That is because a criminal, by definition, is someone who does not obey the law. So you can have all the gun laws you want, they are not going to stop criminals from getting and using guns, as evidenced by places like Chicago and Camden. Furthermore, in a time when criminals, especially gang members, are more armed than ever all these new, tougher laws are doing is keeping firearms out of the hands of law-abiding citizens, thus leaving them more vulnerable to violent crimes. Each year the law-abiding, taxpaying, legal citizens of this nation are becoming more and more defenseless. Of course, that is by design.

Even with myriad of different state and local firearm laws and ordinances across the country it is a perpetuated fallacy that America has the highest murder rate in the civilized world. You have to look no further than our neighbor to the south, Mexico, which despite some of the strictest gun laws on the planet has become a virtual war zone. By some estimates, 85,000 people have been killed in Mexico since 2006, though the exact number is hard to pinpoint because so many thousands of people simply "disappear". For comparison, according to the Organisation for Economic Co-operation and Development (OECD), in 2014, the homicide rate for Mexico (the number of murders per 100,000 inhabitants) was 23.4. The homicide rate for the United States is 5.2. There are some that are quick to say that many of the guns used in killings in Mexico came from the United States. But that in no way supports the notion of tougher gun laws because, other than Operation Fast and Furious where the U.S. government actually purposely gave mostly assault weapons to Mexican drug cartels, all the guns that flow into Mexico are done so illegally and nearly 100% of the guns that are used in Mexico, no matter their origins, are done so illegally.

But it is not just Mexico. Russia also has some of the toughest gun laws on Earth, yet according to the OECD their homicide rate is more than double that of the United States.

Whenever new gun laws are enacted or debated the first thing those who wish to impose them say is "no one wants to go into your house and take your guns away". This has proven to be a lie. In 2005, in the aftermath of Hurricane Katrina, federal and local law enforcement agents forced citizens in some of the most flooded, impacted areas to hand over their legal firearms. At a time when these American citizens were at their most vulnerable and needed their guns for protection they were taken. Of course, the mainstream media mostly buried this story.

The mainstream media, with the exception of editorial shows, is supposed to be unbiased. However, they are unabashedly and radically anti-Second Amendment. They fill their airwaves and Internet sites with anti-gun propaganda, purposely omitting facts, twisting truths, and even fabricating statistics. For instance, you almost never hear the mainstream media reporting on all the times citizens use legally owned firearms to shoot burglars, attackers, and rapists because that would perpetuate the truth that guns actually give law-abiding citizens a way of defending themselves and have saved many lives, and that goes directly against the anti-Second Amendment narrative. Likewise, the major news networks also almost never report on the overwhelming majority of gun deaths, which are gang related, because that proves that gun laws do not prevent criminals from either shooting each other or innocent victims. In addition, sometimes when they do report on a shooting where the perpetrator has obtained the firearm illegally they often conveniently leave out that fact.

The media is great at leaving out facts, as well as not checking details they report as facts. One example of this is that several news stations, such as CNN and MSNBC, trumpeted Michael Bloomberg's anti-gun group's apocalyptic-like statistics as gospel. Columnist and commentator John Lott later showed that several main components of the statistics were either fabricated or at least distorted.

The majority of the time the media gets their facts wrong about gun violence is because they are trying to push the narrative that laws can stop criminals and even legally owned firearms should be banned. But sometimes it is purely out of ignorance. Though I want to be careful not to accuse every news anchor and commentator of this, many of them have never picked up a gun, let alone taken any firearms training, or even cared to learn about firearms. Yet they have no problem spending hours upon hours talking about different firearms. Maybe the best illustration of this is the media's un-relenting obsession with the Bushmaster .223. They have spent countless airtime going on about this particular firearm as if it was the only gun that kills people, or even that Bushmaster is the only manufacturer to make a gun that uses the .223 cartridge. British implant and anti-gun extremist Piers Morgan went as far as to say on his news show one time that the .223 is the most dangerous round in the world. Make no mistake about it, a .223 round is deadly and can kill you, just as a .22 round, but those that know anything about firearms know that most hunting rifles carry a much larger cartridge. In fact, the .223 is one of the smallest long-gun cartridges. Of course, than there are shotguns, which under certain circumstances, can do a lot more damage than someone with an AR-15. However, the main problem with the media's obsessive attack on the .223, AR-15, or all "assault rifles" belies the undeniable fact that the vast majority of gun deaths across the country are committed with handguns.

The media plays a pivotal role in the disarming of America. But perhaps there is no greater conspirator to the destruction of the Second Amendment than celebrities. Clearly, there are staunch Second Amendment and gun rights supporters in Hollywood and pop culture as a whole. But those people are unfortunately drowned out by the minions of anti-gun, anti-Second Amendment extremists in the highest ranks of show business. Many reading this may say "whoa, movies and television shows have more gun violence and are more graphic than ever" and no one can argue that fact. But that just means actors, writers, directors, and producers give new meaning to the word "hypocrite". While making their fortunes on the back of gun violence, they individually spew the most radical anti-gun views imaginable in interviews, articles, and documentaries.

There have been few actors that have ranted their anti-gun sentiments more than Liam Neeson, especially when it comes to America and guns. However, he has no problem making numerous movies where he uses a plethora of various firearms to kill people. Sean Penn, who actually at one time collected guns, changed his views and in 2013 got rid of them all calling them "cowardly killing machines". There is certainly nothing wrong with anyone changing his or her mind or views. However, two years later he starred in the movie The Gunman in which he uses various types of guns to kill people. It may surprise many to know that Sylvester Stallone, who has made such movies as the Rambo franchise and Bullet to the Head, is also self-proclaimed anti-Second Amendment. It is not only actors. One of the biggest movie producers, Harvey Weinstein, who made such movies as Kill Bill, Reservoir Dogs, and Rambo, routinely lambasts the Second Amendment and guns and promised to make the National Rifle Association wish that they had never existed. Still, these are just several examples of the out-of-control hypocrisy awash in Hollywood when it comes to firearms (among many other things).

Maybe even more hypocritical than protesting guns at the same time they make movies glorifying gun violence, many celebrities have bodyguards armed with—you guessed it, guns. So, it is okay for them to be protected by firearms, but not the average law-abiding American citizen.

In case the government, media, and Hollywood are not effective in abolishing the Second Amendment, or at least making people think it is morally wrong, there is always the indoctrination and brainwashing in our schools. In a textbook being used in Texas it has the text of the Bill of Rights. For the Second Amendment it states: "The people have the right to keep and bear arms in a state militia". Of course, this is not what the actual text says. To be clear, the book does not put forth that this is a mere interpretation, but rather the actual text that was ratified. This is no mistake. The Second Amendment is only one sentence long and can easily be found by a simple Google search.

The All Knowing Eye

The Internet and other mobile technology has made many of our lives easier. It is also a vital tool to the Oligarchy's master plan. They may not have foreseen such technology, but they were quick to capitalize on it and expand its uses. Federal agencies like the NSA spy on every part of our lives. They can read our private emails, listen to our phone conversations, see what books we read, what we purchase on line. Through cameras in our computers, mobile phones, and smart TVs, the technology even exists to see what we are doing without us even knowing.

In 2014 the NSA completed its new Utah Data Center. According to the NSA's own website the entire facility is one million square feet, containing twenty different buildings. Though it is officially classified, according to some estimates, like those posted by NPR by an NSA whistleblower, the center will have a storage capacity of five zettabytes. One zettabyte is the equivelant of 1,000,000,000,000 gigabytes. Why would the NSA need such a facility? The answer, which was leaked by NSA contractor Edward Snowden, but can also be explained by the common sense theory that there is no other plausible reason, is so they can collect and store data on almost every American citizen. The irony that the American taxpayers footed the disclosed 1.5 billion dollar bill for the facility cannot be lost.

But it is not just the NSA. In June of 2015, it was publicized that the FBI has its own secret surveillance air force with over one hundred unmarked planes registered under fictitious companies to mask the fact that they belong to the agency. The planes are equipped with electronic surveillance equipment. Once the secretive operation was uncovered, the FBI asserted that they only use the aircraft to track specific suspects. However, the highly sophisticated equipment used can easily monitor and record the various devices of all citizens they fly over. Also, if it was not for the nefarious reason of spying on the general population without warrants, than the planes would not be registered under fake companies. The FBI admits that the reason they register the planes fictitiously is so they cannot be traced back to the agency, but absurdly assert it is because if they were the aircraft would be subject to sabotage. If this was the case than the FBI headquarters and every single field office should be hidden and kept secret.

The FBI's surveillance program is scary enough, but they use their air force of surveillance planes in conjunction with state and local law enforcement authorities. There is also no doubt that state authorities, especially in more densely populated areas, have different electronic surveillance capabilities of their own.

There is no denying that this technology has been used to catch and prosecute criminals and solve otherwise unsolvable crimes. It is also used everyday in the global and never-ending fight against terrorism. The government makes sure to play on the fear that if they are not allowed the ability to monitor people and groups through these means than none of us will be safe. But as Benjamin Franklin said: "Those who surrender freedom for security will not have, nor do they deserve, either one". The same technologies that government agencies use to catch criminals and terrorists are just as much being used everyday to spy on law-abiding American citizens and intrude on their rights protected by the Constitution.

Benjamin Franklin may not have known, nor ever dreamed of, things like the Internet, cell phones, or drones, but the principal is still the same. Even thirty years ago, Americans would have never had put up with government agents entering all our homes without warrants and searching our belongings, or listening to our private conversations. However, that is exactly what is happening today; only instead of physical agents doing the work, it is done electronically. It is even worse, because what they find, intercept, and record can be stored indefinitely.

Even if you think you are off the grid, if you have never been online or used a cell phone in your life, you are still being monitored. Many automobiles now come with the equivalent of "black boxes" able to determine where you have been. If you live in a metropolitan area, every time you use your metro card it is a fingerprint of when and where you used it. If you use a credit card, not only does that merchant hold onto your information, but they often sell your data to third party vendors and certainly the government has access. Then of course, there is the literal eye in the sky. It is hard to go anywhere in this country without being observed and recorded by cameras. They are everywhere: At intersections, on rooftops, in parks, strewn across urban areas. Not only do almost all places of businesses have multiple cameras that record video on hard drives, but some places, such as resorts and bars, even have webcams that anyone can remotely access in real time. Speaking of webcams, almost all computers have them and in what has become a growing trend, hackers have remotely turned on these cameras without the person knowing and spied on individuals, mostly women undressing or in other private moments. However, if opportunistic hackers can do this certainly so can the government. But if fixed cameras are not spying and tracking you there is now the use of drones, which is growing exponentially. Within five years they will probably be everywhere. If the government can track down a goat herder in the mountains of Afghanistan, they can certainly track you.

One cannot talk about today's technology, specifically the Internet, without discussing social media. It is being used by children and grandparents, as well as by law enforcement and terrorists. It crosses by all social and economic classes. Social media is the great paradox. When most people think of sites like Facebook and Twitter they think about free speech. It is the place where anyone can go to state his or her opinions and views, no matter how radical. However, at the same time, those views and opinions are being used to track and categorize us. There is no denying this has been useful in tracking down pedophiles, terrorists, and other nefarious actors. But it is also being used by employers, the government, and other corporate entities to find out and record what we do, where we are, what we like, what we are against, and if we will be compliant to the Oligarchy's plans.

Social media is also a great tool for indoctrination. Government agents posing as "ordinary citizens" troll individuals and groups and spread propaganda. Henchmen for politicians and the Oligarchy do the same thing, creating rumors and outright lies about opposition. With the lightning-speed of the Internet, in no time at all, those lies become truths.

However, it goes beyond spying and indoctrination. It is no secret that the more technologically advanced a civilization is, the easier it is to destroy—or control. Certainly if the Internet was to be shut down, which it can be, most of us would find it extremely inconvenient. But our lives now depend on a vulnerable computer grid. If an individual or group was to hack into, and either shut off or corrupt, certain systems planes would fall from the sky, our electric and water filtration systems would become inoperable, our military and defense systems would not work. Today, one of the biggest threats talked about is cyber warfare, the ability of terrorists or enemy governments to hack into our most important computer systems. This is a real and growing threat. But another threat is the ability of our own government to disguise itself as foreign actors to turn off or damage vital systems in specific areas.

The Caliphate

The powers that be have worked long and hard on their plans for a global oligarchy. However, in the end, their goal may ultimately fall short, but not because of internal resistance from those seeking to preserve democracy. At the same time these magnates are preparing the final stages of their plan to control the world, another group is planning on implementing a global caliphate. Like a virus taking advantage of a weakened immune system, jihadists are seizing on the deterioration of the strength and resolve of America and its European allies.

Not even some of the most oil-rich governments of the Middle East want a caliphate. The Saudi Royal Family, one of the most oppressive regimes there is, who themselves impose sharia law on their people, is adamantly opposed to ISIS and their apocalyptic vision, because it goes against their bottom line. They are also sworn enemies of ISIS. Though the Saudis may like to see the whole world convert to Islam, their ultimate goal, as part of the Oligarchy, is to make more money and keep their influential status on the world stage.

Though the rise of jihad was an unforeseen event, which caught the Oligarchy off guard, they are surely aware of it now. Of course, their first choice is to eradicate it. However, this threat is growing too fast and too strong. If it cannot be defeated, the Oligarchy's plan, which they have been exercising to hedge against a military victory, is appeasement. They know they cannot fight the jihadists and the American citizens at the same time, at least not and win. So their plan is to give the jihadists a little of what they want in hopes that they can be contained. However, in this plan containment has already led to expansion.

It is Neville Chamberlain all over again, when he gave Hitler Czechoslovakia and other concessions believing that he would stop there and not expand his aggressions. In fairness to Chamberlain, many of the world leaders at the time turned their heads to what Hitler and the Nazis were doing, choosing not to intervene in the slight hope that he would somehow contain himself. Of course, history tells us that this plan backfired and actually fed Hitler's aggression and sense of power and supremacy. And as history always repeats itself, the same thing will happen today. However, assured they are smarter than everyone else, including history, the Oligarchy has been in an elaborate and long-term appeasement with the Islamic extremists.

President Obama and members of his Administration have gone out of their way to condemn anyone who slanders Islam, particularly the prophet Mohamed. They vehemently refuse to say that America is at war with Islamic extremism. They even refuse to call ISIS (or ISIL) Islamic, even though the first two letters stand for Islamic State. The government even arrested Nakoula Basseley Nakoula, the man who made an anti-Islamic YouTube video, which they tried to falsely assert was the reason our embassy in Libya was attacked and our ambassador and three other Americans killed. But the appeasement runs much deeper.

At a time when anything to do with Christianity is being forced out of America's schools, Islam is infiltrating textbooks and curriculum. There is a push in several Muslim communities across the nation to implement Sharia law. There was even a long fought battle to include an Islamic exhibit and erect a mosque across the street at the 9/11 Memorial Museum, which of course is a memorial to the all those killed by Islamic extremists on September 11, 2001. That would be like creating a shrine to the Empire of Japan next to the USS Arizona Memorial in

Pearl Harbor. Maybe today some people would even think that is a good idea. But when the Memorial was built that notion would have been so absurd and extreme it would have been condemned by all as heresy.

I want to be perfectly clear that not all Muslims are terrorists. Many of them are peaceful. It is also wrong to indict an entire religion. However, neither the government, nor many in the mainstream media, seem to have any problem with someone slandering Jesus or Christianity, or any other religion. When the Brooklyn Museum displayed a painting by "artist" Chris Ofili of the Virgin Mary covered in elephant feces and with cutouts of genitalia from pornographic magazines in the background, there was an outcry from some in the Christian community, but not from anyone in the government and most of the media actually sided with Ofili, citing his right to express himself as an artist. Then there is artist Andres Serrano, who's exhibit, Piss Christ, a picture of the Crucifix covered in Serrano's urine, was displayed at the Edward Tyler Nahem gallery in New York. The exhibit received no condemnation from the government and only passing mention by a few media outlets. Meanwhile, artists who have depicted the prophet Mohamed have been killed by Islamists, most notoriously the terrorist attack on the French paper Charlie Hebdo, where twelve people were gunned down.

The government's vehement condemnation, and in certain cases, even punishment for individuals or groups that are even perceived to slander Islam goes further than the issue of appeasement. It goes against the First Amendment, which protects American's freedom of speech.

Islamic groups are committing genocide across the globe. Despite President Obama's assertion to the contrary, the one thing that the all of the most perilous terrorist groups now spreading death across the world—ISIS, Al-Qeada, Abu Sayyaf, Al-Shabaab, Boko Haram—have in common is that they are not only Islamic, but are killing in the name of the Quran. There is no doubting that all these groups kill fellow Muslims too, mostly because they believe they are not adherent enough to Islam. But their main objective is to commit genocide on non-Muslims, people of different faith, especially Christians and Jews. In various attacks, such as the Westgate Mall massacre in Kenya, terrorists asked people if they were Muslim and even asked some to recite verses from the Quran. Those who were not Muslim were killed.

Though there are numerous murderous Islamic organizations the most notorious and dangerous is the Islamic State or ISIS or ISIL. They are rapidly spreading like an out of control cancer and committing killings, rapes, and tortures on a biblical scale. Taking over swaths of entire countries they, above all, are hell-bent on a caliphate and an apocalyptic dream. But the current Administration continues to downplay their significance and threat to the world. To go back to the comparison of the Nazis, generations that came after asked in disbelief how the rest of the world sat back and let Hitler come to power and almost achieve his psychotic vision of the eradication of the Jews and global domination. Rest assure that if the Islamic State is not confronted with full force and defeated, future generations will ask the same question of us. But though the powers that be are using the historically failed strategy of appeasement, just as Chamberlain and many other leaders used when Hitler was coming to power, the difference is that even by the time Hitler invaded Poland the true scope of the Nazis atrocities were not yet known. Though Hitler's views on the Jews were known, the Final Solution would not be officially implemented until 1941, after Britain had already declared war on Germany. Even many of the Nazis' war crimes before that had been at least tried to be kept secret by the Reich. In comparison, ISIS purposely films and airs their genocide for the entire world to see.

Though the Islamic State's genocide has not yet reached the United States—at least not at the time of this book's printing—it is their goal. It is coming if we do not defeat them. The Oligarchy within our government, and those in our government beholden to the Oligarchy, must stop their strategy of appeasement, stop focusing on controlling law-abiding American citizens, and concentrate all their efforts into defeating ISIS. As I previously stated, appeasement of the caliphate will put an end to the Oligarchy anyway. ISIS has stated that they wish to raise "the flag of Allah" on top of the White House. That day may very well come. Of course, there are those that say that it already has.

Contingency Plans

E ven with indoctrination, the tireless propaganda of division, and the great effort to disarm the populace, there will still be pockets of resistance. But the government has plans in place to knock out these pockets, by using various federal agencies to target individuals and groups, not just by shear force, but also by intimidation and covert operations.

There is no more powerful federal agency involved in the everyday lives of American citizens than the Internal Revenue Service. They can ruin your personal life and/or business just as much as a gunshot or a bomb. Though there are a façade of procedures in place for hearings and recourse, if they go after you it is David vs. Goliath and the vast majority of the time, unlike David, you do not even have a stone. In the extremely rare event that you do stave-off or win your case against the IRS you will probably go bankrupt in the process. Most of the time the damage is already done.

It has been proven that the IRS is being used as a weapon of mass destruction against tax-paying American citizens and their businesses. It was discovered that starting in 2010 (that we know about) the IRS specifically targeted numerous conservative groups by auditing them, miring them in insurmountable paperwork, and refusing to approve their exempt status, making some groups concentrate all their efforts on fighting the IRS and rendering others basically inoperable. By the time this crime came to light Barrack Obama was already elected for a second term and thus no matter what happened afterwards the IRS, or more importantly those instructing the IRS, had already achieved their goal.

Of course, at first both the IRS and the Administration blamed the targeting on a few rogue agents in the Cincinnati office. Still, when it was shown to be much more wide spread, the cover-up machine went into full gear and no one was ever held accountable. Louis Lerner, the then Director of the Exempt Organizations Unit of the IRS was brought before Congress, but simply pleaded the Fifth. When asked to provide Lerner's emails regarding the subject, the IRS used the ludicrous excuse that it had lost all of Lerner's emails due to a computer crash— an excuse that would never work if a taxpayer tried to use it against the IRS. But the excuse did work because the IRS is above any law.

On a smaller scale, but still frightening and un-Constitutional, President Richard Nixon used the IRS to target left wing and anti-war groups, mostly making them go through unnecessary and inappropriate audits.

Sitting Presidents using the overwhelming power of the IRS to attack their opponents and groups with which they do not agree is alarming in itself and should put fear, rage, and disgust into every American citizen. Not to mention it goes against everything for which Democracy stands. But these are just two examples of the IRS acting as a tyrannical group that were so widespread and grand that they became public knowledge (and still the IRS was not held accountable). What about the smaller, more pinprick targeting that no doubt the IRS conducts everyday? It has already been shown by the Obama and Nixon administrations that the IRS can be controlled by higher, outside sources. The Oligarchy, be it directly or indirectly through their government pawns, surely has the IRS in their holster. During Obama's second presidential campaign the IRS searched for words and phrases such as "Tea Party", "Patriots", and "Government Debt" within forms and requests to help target anti-Obama groups. So they can definitely do it again with the same or different terms. Even more terrifying is that, in conjunction with the NSA, they can target individuals and groups that use certain terms, or fit certain profiles, based on personal emails or social media postings.

As destructive and powerful as the IRS is, it is not the only tool for crushing pockets of resistance. Many point to the wide powers granted to the Federal Emergency Management Agency (FEMA). Many of the services FEMA provides are vital to aiding communities after a natural or manmade disaster. One of the services they provide is setting up camps for displaced individuals. The government should give shelter to those who have had their homes destroyed. However, countless individuals who have stayed in these camps, like those set up after Hurricane Katrina, say they are more like prisons, with guards and encirclements of barbwire that face inward. Though it is the topic of great debate of fact versus fiction, there have even been numerous reports that FEMA even has empty camps already set-up within America, ready to use at a moments notice. It would be easy for FEMA to capitalize on a disaster—some say they already have—but is the agency just doing dry runs for a future internment of American citizens? Manmade disasters can come in various shapes and sizes and their true origins concealed.

But it is not just FEMA. After the Boston Bombings in 2013, in pursuit of the remaining suspect, local and federal law enforcement agencies basically took over the entire city and suburbs. There was a dangerous terrorist on the loose and police were prudent to search for him cautiously, while at the same time protecting the public. However, many saw the vast amount of officers and equipment, rolling down public streets, going into houses and businesses, as an overreach and saw into a window of what it would look like if governmental forces were deployed to control a population for more sinister reasons.

The government also maintains a large stockpile of the deadliest diseases and agents known to man, from anthrax to bubonic plague, from SARS to Hantavirus. They can potentially use these invisible killers to crush any pockets of resistance. If you think that the government unleashing diseases and committing other covert operations on its own citizens is pure paranoia and could never happen you are wrong, because it already has. In 1995 President Clinton officially apologized for secret radiation experiments that were conducted by the federal government upon U.S. citizens from 1944 all the way to 1974. As one part of the experiment, hospital patients were unknowingly injected with plutonium to determine how long the substance would remain in their bodies. In the 1960's the Army secretly released a variant of the bacteria bacillus subtilis throughout the New York City subway system in order to track how many people would be infected. It was estimated that one million commuters were exposed. Though the Army later claimed that the bacteria was harmless and no one became ill, they also said that they did not monitor any of the individuals who were exposed. One of the most well known of government experiments was the Tuskegee Syphilis Study, where hundreds of impoverished black males were tricked into volunteering after being told they had "bad blood", which at the time referred to a host of different ailments. In fact, the men had been diagnosed with syphilis—though they were never told—which the experiment was meant to study. The experiment ran from the 1930's to 1972. Although penicillin was found to treat syphilis in 1947, none of the subjects were ever told or given penicillin.

Can We Be Saved?

Throughout this book I have used several quotes from our Founding Fathers and other great Americans because I believe they are important and pertinent. But perhaps no quote is more pertinent than this one from President Ronald Reagan: "Freedom is never more than one generation away from extinction. We didn't pass it to our children in the bloodstream. It must be fought for, protected, and handed on for them to do the same." Perhaps when Reagan made this speech he was thinking mostly of outside forces, such as Communism. But today, and maybe it has been this way from the beginning, though we force formidable and dangerous foreign forces, our greatest threat comes from within. Terrorists may destroy our buildings. Someday maybe rouge nations will even destroy an entire city. But when our Constitution, when our freedoms and rights, are taken away our entire nation is destroyed.

The only reason we still have any freedoms in America is because of the sweat, blood, and lives of countless brave men and women who have worn the uniform, as well as the great sacrifices made by their families, from the Revolutionary War to the War of 1812; from World War I to World War II; from Korea to Vietnam; from Iraq to Afghanistan. We the People must fight with our dying breath to preserve our freedom and the

American Dream, for ourselves, but also so that all the generations of veterans gave was not given in vain.

But though us civilians must fight this fight, the time may come when we must call upon our brothers and sisters in the armed forces. Soldiers follow orders, no matter how dangerous and how much they may disagree. It is the only way a military structure works and throughout the years they have done so with immense valor. It is part of what has made us, and still makes us, the most formidable and valiant military in the world. But if the time ever comes when those that so bravely wear our nation's uniform are asked to turn their weapons and use force against their own citizens they must step across the line and stand on the side of the People. Though they heroically go wherever they are asked to go, do whatever they are asked to do, they are ultimately there to defend the People, even from our own government. After all, these great men and women are part of us, the People.

Besides, time and time again, especially in recent years, the government has mistreated our veterans, from the horrid conditions uncovered at Walter Reed National Medical Center to the fraudulent waiting lists veterans were forced to wait on for medical treatment at Phoenix VA Hospital and others, resulting in numerous deaths. Despite selflessly and heroically following the governments' orders, the government has treated our troops like second-class citizens once they return home. But it is not just our government. Fortune 500 companies, such as JP Morgan Chase, have been caught defrauding military members and their families.

Recently, there has been a widespread push to label the majority of police officers as rouge, out-of-control racists who have no regard for citizens. Not only is this untrue, but it is extremely dangerous. The overwhelming majority of policemen and women are righteous and trying to do a very difficult, precarious, and often thankless job. But most importantly, we need the rank-and-file police. If it was not for them there would be daily anarchy in the streets and no one would be safe. We also need them, if the time should ever come, to stand on the side of the People against forced tyranny. Everyone knows the law enforcement slogan: To Protect and Serve. That means to protect and serve the citizens of the community, not to protect and serve the government or some other powerful entity. But even more important is the oath every police officer must take. Though the exact oath may vary from state to state, there is always a provision that the officer must obey and defend the Constitution of the United States. It is upon this oath that police officers must take up sides with the law-abiding citizens of the country against any unconstitutional and unjust governmental force.

I also implore those that may be agents or contractors of the Oligarchy to help defend democracy and the Constitution. I am sure there are those individuals that may be working in the DOJ, NSA, IRS, FBI, CIA, and other agencies that are not only aware of unconstitutional operations and activities, but are opposed to them. Maybe the things they know even keep them up at night. However, they do not speak out or take any actions because they are afraid of retribution to themselves, as well as their families. It is understandable human nature to protect oneself and noble to want to protect one's family. It is also logical to want to protect one's career. However, I ask these individuals what if they, or their families, were the targets of these nefarious operations? What if they were being spied on, violated, or having their rights or property taken? First off, unless they are at the very top of the totem pole, they are as expendable as the rest of us. They are also easy to become scapegoats. Furthermore, though some of these individuals may think if you can't beat them join them, do they really want their children and grandchildren growing up in a tyranny? I beseech them to take a stand, to speak out, to bring to light any unconstitutional and nefarious plans or acts.

In the end, however, it is up to every citizen to fight for his or her own freedoms. We must fight for our liberties in the face of persecution, imprisonment, and even death. But we cannot wait for some impeding conflict where force must be met with force. The whole point of this book is to outline the fact that our freedoms are not being taken away by force. Many of our rights and liberties as Americans have already been confiscated, not by armed intervention, but by closed-door meetings and the mere use of a pen.

We The People are the last American stronghold, the last line of defense against the ultimate collapse of our Constitution and the complete implementation of utter tyranny. The People have rights granted to us under the Constitution and its amendments. It is those rights that make us American and make the idea and dream of democracy a reality. So we must fight for those rights, even by force if necessary. To do so is not unlawful. To the contrary, it is the most judicial and noble thing we can do. We must do this not only for ourselves, but even more importantly, for our children, their children, and all those who follow us. Otherwise, future generations will grow up in a place they used to call America.

www.ingramcontent.com/pod-product-compliance
Lightning Source LLC
Chambersburg PA
CBHW050339290526
45785CB00006B/2564